It's a Small Town If ...

PHOTOGRAPHS AND PERCEPTIONS
BY SAM BRECK

HEARTLAND PRESS
AN IMPRINT OF NORTHWORD PRESS, INC.

Acknowledgments

THANKS to the many who, through their encouragement and forbearance, helped to make this little book what it is, or at least what it appears to be. Among the specially honored are Marion Breck (proof- and copy-reader), Bob and Bill Breck, whose patience has been inexhaustible, and Bertie Bonnell, Howard Thompson, Dean Arnold, and Sharon Balius. Brenda Renyard's darkroom talents produced the prints, and the excellent, dependable cameras pioneered by Oscar Barnack made the photographs possible.

Photographs

The photographs were made in these places:

Michigan—Blissfield, Byron, Chelsea, Dundee, Durand, East Jackson, Gregory, Marion, Milford, Perry, Saline, Shepherd, South Lyon, Stockbridge

Indiana—Angola, Atlanta, Arcadia, Butler, Corunna, Glenwood, Hamilton, Markle, North Manchester, North Vernon, Sweetser, Waterloo

Illinois—Onarga, Sheldon

Ohio—Hayesville, Pettisville, St. Henry, Stryker, Wauseon

There's also one photograph from someplace in Kentucky.

Cover photograph: Jasper, Arkansas

Library of Congress Cataloging-in-Publication Data

Breck, Samuel L. , 1928-
   [It's a small town]
   It's a small town if-- / by Samuel L. Breck , Jr.
      p.   cm.
   Originally published under the title: It's a small town.
   ISBN 1-55971-147-7 : $6.95
    1. City and town life–United States. 2. City and town
life--Middle West. 3. United States–Social life and customs–1971-
4. Middle West--Social life and customs. I. Title.
E169.04.B74 1993
973'.09732–dc20
                       92-43517
                       CIP

Published by: Heartland Press, an imprint of NorthWord Press, Inc.,
P.O. Box 1360, Minocqua, WI 54548

For a free catalog describing NorthWord's line of nature books
and gift items, call 1-800-336-5666.

ISBN 1-55971-147-7

Printed in the United States of America

Introduction

They're writing obituaries for small towns.

The nation's heavy thinkers—the sociologists, psychologists, and assorted other -ologists—are doomsaying, predicting that the American small town is a goner. We'd better act soon, they imply, and use some government money to preserve our towns in museums.

If it comes to that, I'll suggest putting a small town on the Mall outside the Smithsonian, where the politicians and social engineers, whose vision of small-town life comes from flying 30,000 feet overhead, will be reminded that a lot of the country's real strength is found in its little communities. In fact, the Inaugural Parade might be re-routed down the town's Main Street, right past the Dari-Dip store and the Koin Kleen laundromat.

Don't believe the folks with letters after their names. The small town is as alive as any place. It simply lacks the exhaust, the noise, and the squeeze-and-shove lifestyles that are epidemic in larger places. Just because there's no interstate exit at its door doesn't mean a town is ready to be donated to the archaeologists. In fact, its isolation probably ensures its health. Chamber of Commerce types may harrumph at this notion, but they're followers of the dogma that change and congestion are always better and "good for the economy." What else would you expect from people who think only of super-somethings and high-tech industrial parks? What's good for *people* doesn't seem to concern them.

Admittedly, I'm addicted to little places, and although you may not be a terminal case like me, just the fact that you're holding this book indicates that you probably have a touch of envy, nostalgia, or curiosity about small towns. You probably also understand that the towns don't all look alike. If you're doubtful, visit a few each year and, in time, you'll be able to actually *see* small towns, not just look at them. You'll discover those delightful idiosyncracies that make small places interesting and different. If you give it a sincere try, you may even find them fascinating.

So, angle-park your car on Main in front of the Western Auto, and take a slow-paced stroll down to the corner of Depot, then hang a left, cross the tracks to Mill, double back on Maple, Madison, Church, and School. Keep listening as well as looking. Small towns have a sound all their own. The sound of things growing, not expiring. The distant, useful sounds of tractors and trains. Tires on wet brick streets. And soft speech:

"Howdy."

"Mornin', Don."

"Hope you'll be at the Guild on Wednesday, Louise."

"See my dad's new Chevy?"

"Come back and see us again, ya hear? And have a nice day."

It's a small town...

 if from where it begins, you can see where it ends.

if visitors are always asking, "What's there to *do* around here, anyhow?"

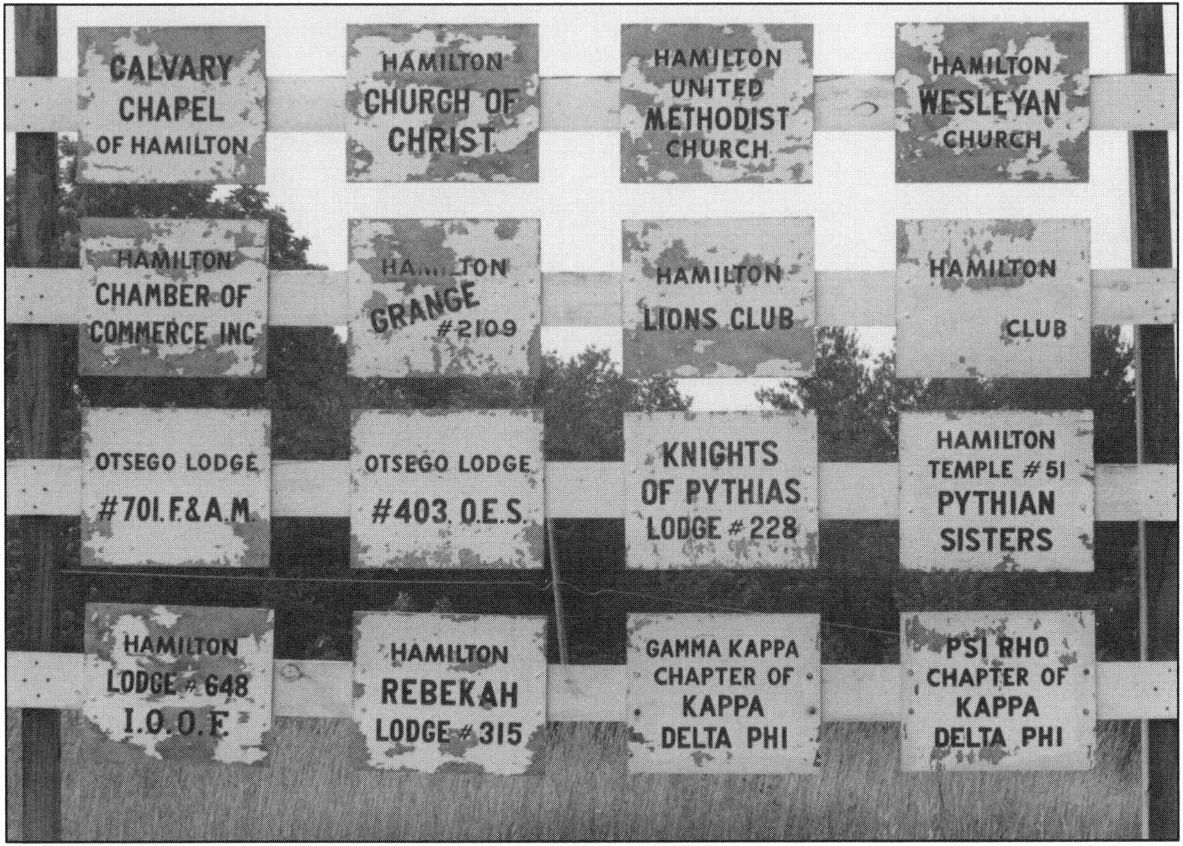

CALVARY CHAPEL OF HAMILTON
HAMILTON CHURCH OF CHRIST
HAMILTON UNITED METHODIST CHURCH
HAMILTON WESLEYAN CHURCH
HAMILTON CHAMBER OF COMMERCE INC
GRANGE #2109
HAMILTON LIONS CLUB
HAMILTON CLUB
OTSEGO LODGE #701. F.&A.M.
OTSEGO LODGE #403. O.E.S.
KNIGHTS OF PYTHIAS LODGE #228
HAMILTON TEMPLE #51 PYTHIAN SISTERS
HAMILTON LODGE #648 I.O.O.F.
HAMILTON REBEKAH LODGE #315
GAMMA KAPPA CHAPTER OF KAPPA DELTA PHI
PSI RHO CHAPTER OF KAPPA DELTA PHI

if there's angle parking on Main Street.

if the well-worn joke about the cemetery is, "We don't need a fence around it, 'cause nobody wants to get in and for sure nobody's gettin' out."

if, at first look, the Zip Code seems the only thing unique about the place.

❖ _____

if there's always a wreath at the base of
the war monument.

if the selection isn't so great, but the *service* brings you back.

if the bank closes early on Wednesday or Thursday afternoon.

if the signs are more functional than promotional.

if it's hard to get a date Wednesday evening because anyone you'd like to go out with has choir practice.

if you don't have to feed a quarter to the air pump.

 if the food store also sells veterinary supplies.

if the motel room comes with a
Gideon Bible and a flyswatter.

if old houses are called just that—not "landmarks" or "architecturally significant structures."

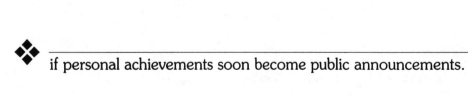 if personal achievements soon become public announcements.

if the traffic signal at the main intersection is a blinker light.

if most of the streets are named for trees, presidents, compass directions, ordinal numbers, or members of your family.

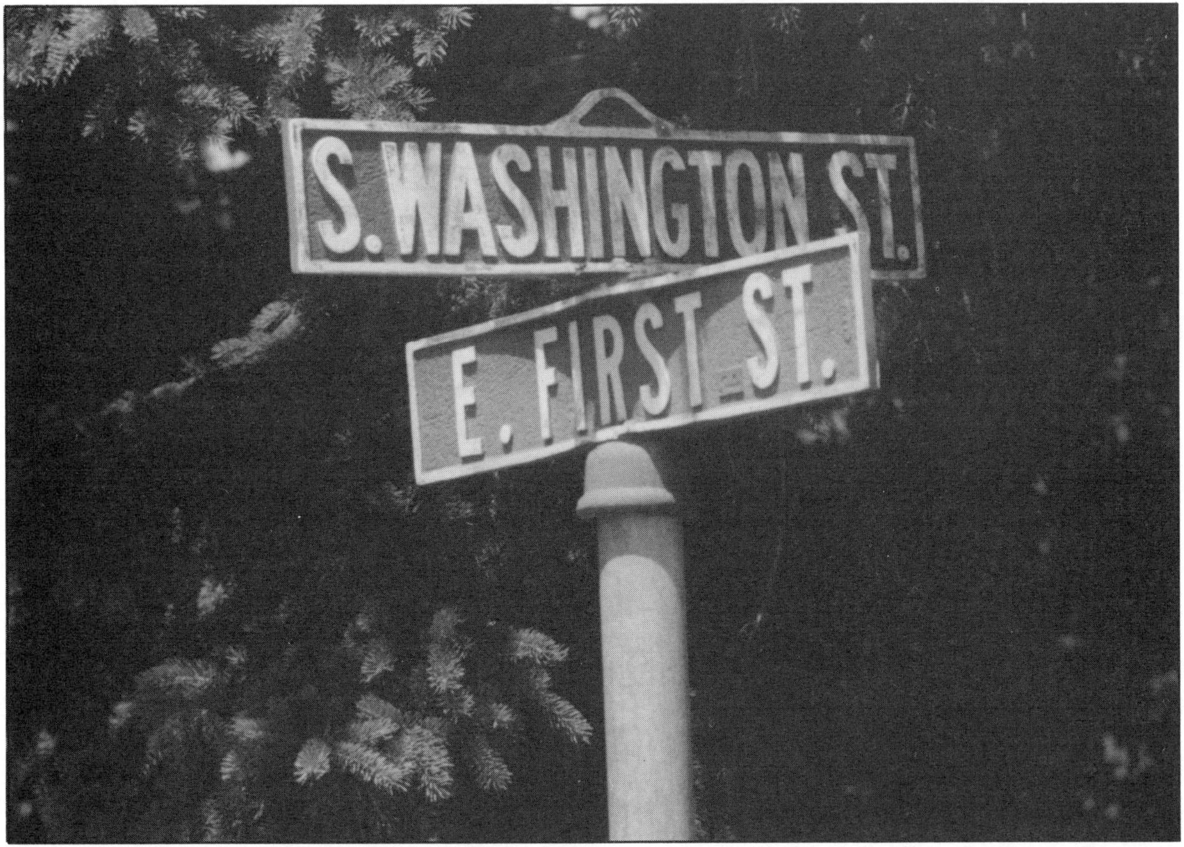
S. WASHINGTON ST.
E. FIRST ST.

if the Legion or the VFW uses artillery as a lawn ornament.

if, in the evening, you can hear a dog bark two blocks away—and know whose dog it is.

if "the show" offers movies (not films) and is open only on weekends.

if the hardware store will sell you one bolt or one nut at a time.

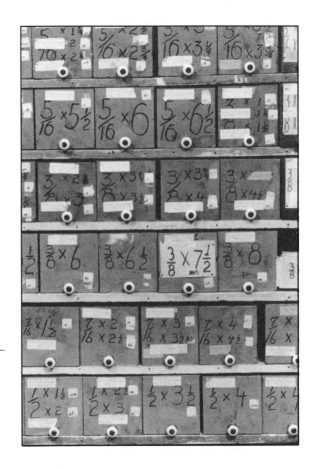

if a look at the waterworks is an essential part of the tour.

if the place doesn't take itself all *that* seriously.

A TOWN WITH A
HISTORY AND A FUTURE

MARKLE

HOME OF 971 HAPPY PEOPLE
AND 4 GROUCHES

if there's not much to see, but what you overhear makes up for it.

if a penny buys some time on the meter.

if the drive-in is owned by a neighbor, not managed by a
computer in the next state.

if government is accessible—and even friendly.

if business can wait when it's time for dinner.

if you get your hair cut (not "styled") in a one-chair shop where you can read *Sports Illustrated, Outdoor Life,* and *Popular Mechanics.*

if, during the summer festival, the volunteer firefighters get thoroughly soaked—
and so does everyone else.

if community triumphs are announced at the town line.

if folks think that growth is a good thing, but maybe it ought to wait until there are more folks in town to make it worthwhile.

if you generally find split pea soup on Thursday's menu at the cafe, and Friday's special is likely to be tuna noodle casserole.

if Sunday is what Sunday was.

if so many folks march in the parade that not many are left to watch it from the curb.

if the IGA's downtown.

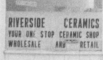

if last Friday's high school game makes page one of this week's paper.

if the train doesn't stop here anymore.

if, when you come back for the annual homecoming celebration, your first view of the skyline is always a little exciting.

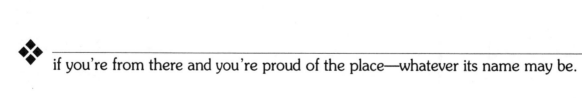

if you're from there and you're proud of the place—whatever its name may be.

About the Author

SAM BRECK, the author and photographer of this book, lives in either a large town or a small city in the Midwest. When he travels in that region in his "real job" as a self-employed promotional specialist, he usually follows the black and blue lines on the map, avoiding the interstates if at all possible. On a Sunday afternoon, he has been known to spend an enjoyable four hours on the main street of a town of 400, while most of the local citizens are out of town visiting. The local folks who stayed home—and the visiting Mr. Breck—enjoy the peace and the quiet. The author's previous books include *Holier Than Thou*, published in 1985.